The Trial of Standing Bear

A special story for the special Goldbergs!

Frank Keating
2009

Made Possible By:

A T & T
Clay & Louise Bennett
Clement & Betty Collogan
Patti Evans
Ike & Mary Beth Glass
Martha Griffin
Frank & Cathy Keating
John McLaughlin
David & Sara Myers
Carl & Carolyn Renfro
The Standing Bear Foundation

ISBN 1-885596-73-1
ISBN 978-1-885596-73-4
Library of Congress Number 2008932828

© Copyright 2008
Oklahoma Heritage Association
Paintings copyright Mike Wimmer—I Do Art, Inc.

Design by Skip McKinstry

Printed by Baker Group, LLC
& Jostens, Inc. - 405.503.3207

OKLAHOMA HERITAGE ASSOCIATION
1400 Classen Drive
Oklahoma City, OK 73106
888.501.2059

The Trial of Standing Bear

By Frank Keating

Paintings by Mike Wimmer

Editor: Gini Moore Campbell

OKLAHOMA HERITAGE | Association

NEBRASKA

KANSAS

INDIAN
TERRITORY

----- MAY - JULY 1877
Ponca removal to Indian Territory

1878
Ponca Indian moved to second reservation.

---- JANUARY 1879
Twenty-nine Poncas flee reservation to
Nebraska with Standing Bear to bury his son.
Arrested March 23, 1879

Standing Bear was a chief, a leader of his people, a wise and noble man, tall in stature and dignified in manner.

He was a Ponca Chief, dressed in a shirt of blue flannel, with collar and cuffs of red cloth, ornamented with brass buttons. His smock was buckskin and a wide belt of beadwork circled his waist.

His calves were wrapped in leggings of blue and upon his feet were moccasins of deer skin.

Around his shoulders was draped a red and blue blanket. Around his neck hung a necklace made from the claws of a grizzly bear.

The year was 1877. Standing Bear and his people had been driven from their land along the banks of the Niobrara River in northeast Nebraska. The white man had given their lands to others. The land always had been their land, a part of themselves. Their soul. Their spirit.

"This is my land," Standing Bear proclaimed, "the Great Father (the President of the United States) did not give it to me. My people were here and owned this land before there was any Great Father...This is mine. God gave it to me."

But his words were not heard. He and his people must leave their homes.

The soldiers formed a line at the end of the village and drove the Indians out. Many hundreds of them. Men, women, children. All were forced to march south.

They carried little with them. The soldiers took their tools, their seed, and much of their household goods. They promised them that a good life would await them in the "warm lands," the Indian Territory, what is now Oklahoma.

But it was not to be.

When they arrived in Indian Territory there was no shelter. No food. The water was bad. The people needed clothing to bear the cold of winter and the heat of summer. Many fell sick. Nearly one in five died. Including Standing Bear's daughter and son.

"I was like a child," Standing Bear said, "I could not even help myself, much less help them."

It was a time of tears and trial. That winter, Standing Bear and twenty-six others decided to reclaim their land. To stand and return. To go home to Nebraska. To return the bones of his son, Bear Shield, to the ground beside the Swift Running Water.

With one spring wagon, three covered wagons, and $20 in cash, they headed north.

"I resolved at last that I would make an attempt to save the lives of a few," Standing Bear said.

Northward they pushed. Assisted by caring white settlers and their Indian friends, the small band of Poncas made it home after ten weeks of toil and hunger and cold.

They were promptly arrested. They had dared to leave their forced home to the south.

"Take pity on me," Standing Bear cried, "Help me to save the lives of the women and children. My brothers, a power which I cannot resist

What followed was one of the remarkable events in American law. Two determined attorneys represented Standing Bear and his band in federal court. They argued that Indians were "men" not "brutes" that the law was bound to respect.

Across the divide that separated red man and white man stepped these two courageous lawyers, Andrew J. Poppleton and John L. Webster. Prodding them and encouraging them were Omaha newspaperman, Henry Tibbles, and Army General George Crook, a fearless Indian fighter and admired soldier.

Would this case be any different? Could an Indian even appear in a Federal court? What legal standard would apply to Indians? Would they be denied the most basic of rights? Could they be "persons" protected by law?

Standing Bear's lawyers argued that Indians were people entitled to all the protections of federal law. Freedom to travel. Freedom to farm. Freedom to live in peace with all men.

The government lawyer argued that Indians had no such rights. They could be told to go and that they should go. They could be told to stay and that they should stay.

When the case was over and the judge prepared to leave the courtroom to make his decision, Standing Bear rose.

He was not expected to speak. But he did. His views were not supposed to be heard, but they were.

And the result was electrifying.

"(My) hand is not the color of yours," Standing Bear said. "But if I pierce it, I shall feel pain. If you pierce your hand, you also feel pain. The blood that will flow from mine will be the same color as yours. I am a man. God made us both."

Standing Bear told the law as it should be. One law for all the people. One people under law. But he was not finished.

Standing Bear turned and looked outside at the spring sky and the new life that coursed through the land.

"I seem to stand on the bank of a river. My wife and little girl are beside me. In front, the river is wide and impassable, and behind there are perpendicular cliffs. No man of my race ever stood there before. There is no tradition to guide me."

"A flood has begun to rise around us. I look despairingly at the great cliffs. I see a steep, stony way leading upward. I grasp the hand of my child. My wife follows. I lead the way up the sharp rocks, while the waters still rise behind us. Finally, I see a rift in the rocks. I feel the prairie breeze strike my cheek."

"I turn to my wife and child with a shout that we are saved! We will return to the Swift Running Water that pours down between the green islands. There are the graves of my fathers. There again we will pitch our teepees and build our fires."

"But a man bars the passage. He is a thousand times more powerful than I. Behind him, I see soldiers as numerous as leaves on the trees. They will obey that man's orders. I too must obey his orders. If he says that I cannot pass, I cannot. The long struggle will have been in vain. My wife and child and I must return and sink beneath the flood. We are weak and faint and sick. I cannot fight."

lowly, he turned and with a look of sorrow and surrender, he faced the judge, and said in a firm voice, "You are that man."